A Guide to
Bodmin Jail and its History

by

Bill Johnson

Published by Bodmin Town Museum, Mount Folly, Bodmin, Cornwall, PL31 2HQ

The Title

The institution for criminals in Bodmin has been known as: Bodmin Gaol; the County Gaol, Cornwall; H M Prison at Bodmin; and Bodmin Jail. The latter spelling has been chosen as the book title for two reasons, firstly, the Act of Parliament, published in 1778, was entitled *'An Act for building an additional Jail...'* and, secondly, in recent times, the *Jail* spelling has been used for the night club and later the tourist attraction and restaurant. Throughout the book the alternate spelling, *gaol,* has been used as this is the most common spelling in published documents.

Published by:
Bodmin Town Museum, Mount Folly, Bodmin, Cornwall, PL31 2HQ.
Manuscript prepared for publication by W H & J M Johnson, the publishing team.
ISBN 978-0-9549913-9-5
Printed by Mid Cornwall Printing, Truro, Cornwall

Contents

To the Keeper of the Gate

To my well beloved friend, Greetings!

Sir, I beseech thee to welcome and protect the bearer of this letter, whom I commend to thee.

Pray, let thine warders and servants give the bearer all accord, shelter and protection from the murderers, thieves, ruffians and spirits that abide in this establishment.

I also confirm that the bearer is a suitable person to be allowed to visit the Jail Tavern to partake of food and ale at a fair price.

Your most humble servant and friend,

James Chapple
Governor of Bodmin Jail
In the Year of Our Lord 1779

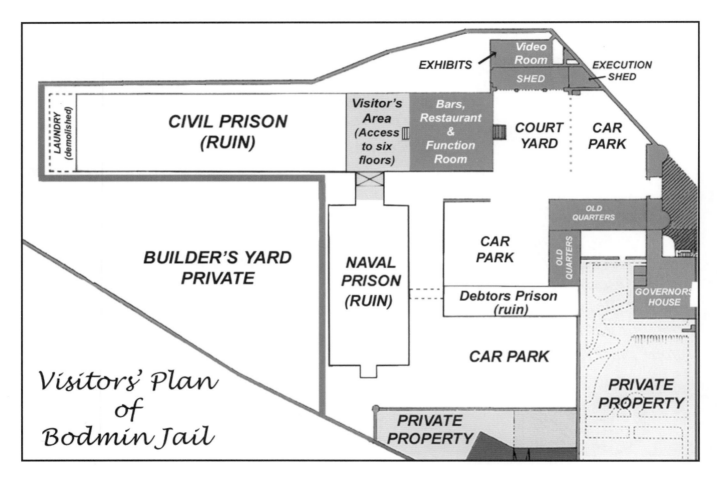

Visitors' Plan of Bodmin Jail

Aerial View of Buildings

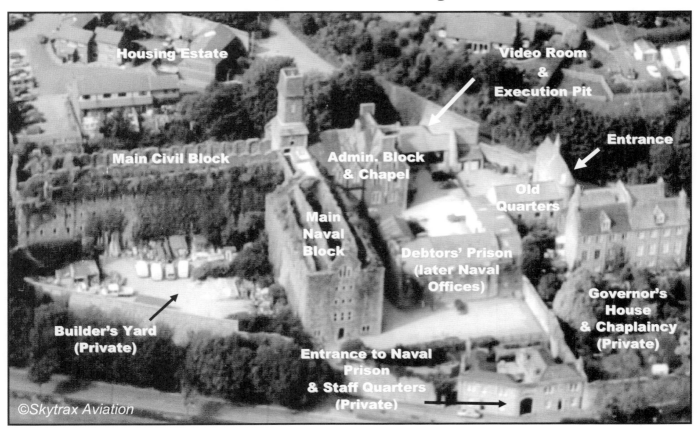

Housing Estate

Video Room & Execution Pit

Main Civil Block

Admin. Block & Chapel

Entrance

Old Quarters

Main Naval Block

Debtors' Prison (later Naval Offices)

Builder's Yard (Private)

Governor's House & Chaplaincy (Private)

Entrance to Naval Prison & Staff Quarters (Private)

©Skytrax Aviation

Details of the Buildings (1)

Main Gate & Gatehouse.
Old quarters can be seen through the archway

Main Office Block   The **Chapel** on the first floor.

The **Main Male Prison Block**

The **Debtors Prison**. After 1887, it
was used as Offices, Stores &
Infirmary by the **Naval Prison.**

The Female Block, later
HM Naval Prison

8

Details of the Buildings (2)

The **Governor's House and Chaplaincy** (photographed from the back)

Goods Hoist

The **Gatehouse** and **Quarters** (**Naval Prison**)

The **Staff Quarters**. A similar building was on the other side of the entrance.

Inside the **Plenum Tower.**

Punishment Cells in the basement

Floor Plans (Levels 3 to 6)

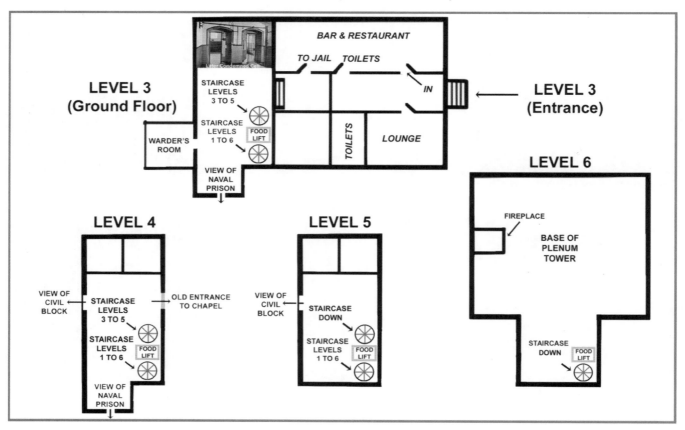

LEVEL 3 (Ground Floor)

Later Condemned Cell

STAIRCASE LEVELS 3 TO 5

STAIRCASE LEVELS 1 TO 6

FOOD LIFT

WARDER'S ROOM

VIEW OF NAVAL PRISON

BAR & RESTAURANT

TO JAIL   TOILETS

IN

TOILETS

LOUNGE

LEVEL 3 (Entrance)

LEVEL 4

VIEW OF CIVIL BLOCK

STAIRCASE LEVELS 3 TO 5

STAIRCASE LEVELS 1 TO 6

FOOD LIFT

OLD ENTRANCE TO CHAPEL

VIEW OF NAVAL PRISON

LEVEL 5

VIEW OF CIVIL BLOCK

STAIRCASE DOWN

STAIRCASE LEVELS 1 TO 6

FOOD LIFT

LEVEL 6

FIREPLACE

BASE OF PLENUM TOWER

STAIRCASE DOWN

FOOD LIFT

Floor Plans (Levels 1 & 2)

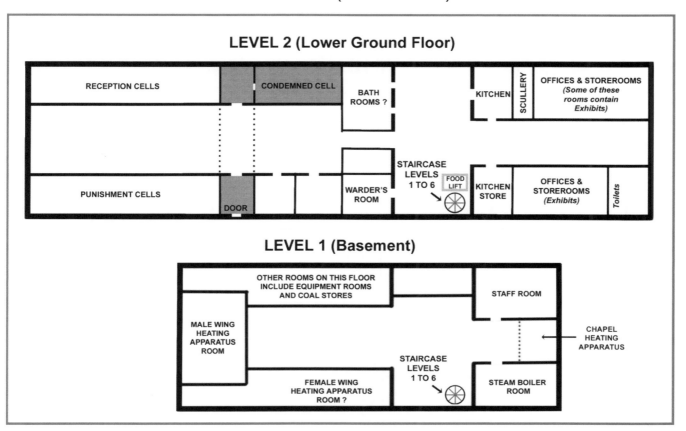

LEVEL 2 (Lower Ground Floor)

RECEPTION CELLS

CONDEMNED CELL

BATH ROOMS ?

KITCHEN

SCULLERY

OFFICES & STOREROOMS
(Some of these rooms contain Exhibits)

PUNISHMENT CELLS

DOOR

WARDER'S ROOM

STAIRCASE LEVELS 1 TO 6

FOOD LIFT

KITCHEN STORE

OFFICES & STOREROOMS
(Exhibits)

Toilets

LEVEL 1 (Basement)

OTHER ROOMS ON THIS FLOOR INCLUDE EQUIPMENT ROOMS AND COAL STORES

STAFF ROOM

MALE WING HEATING APPARATUS ROOM

CHAPEL HEATING APPARATUS

FEMALE WING HEATING APPARATUS ROOM ?

STAIRCASE LEVELS 1 TO 6

STEAM BOILER ROOM

Heating & Ventilation System

1

Hot Air Outlet

Cold Air Inlets

Above: Left-hand side of Stove room
Above Centre: Right-hand side hot Air Outlet
Right: Coal shute?

Top: Smoke pipe going through wall to flue.
Bottom: Inspection hatch in corridor showing the smoke flue.

2

Position of warm-air Duct (from basement below to floor above)

3

Warm-air Inlet

4

Fresh-air Inlet

Stale-air Outlet

5

Have you seen these parts of the Heating System?

1. The stove room in the basement (Level 1).

2. The warm-air duct on the lower ground floor (Level 2).

3. The hollow floor of the main block (view from Level 4).

4. The Inlets and outlets in each cell.

5. The plenum tower, which was the flue for the smoke and the stale air from the cells.

Free Attractions at Bodmin Jail

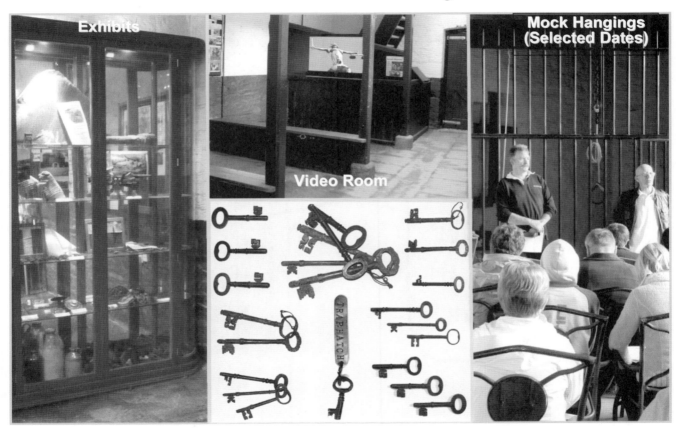

In this section we cover the History of the County Gaol at Bodmin, later known as H.M. Civil Prison.

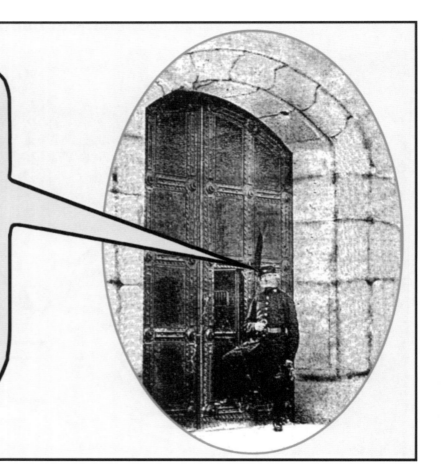

State of the Gaols in Cornwall (before 1776)

COUNTY GAOL AT LAUNCESTON for felons.

The Prison is a room and three Dungeons. They are all very offensive. Their provision is put down to them through a hole in the floor of the room above.

FALMOUTH TOWN GAOL.

Two rooms: no court-yard: no water

TRURO TOWN GAOL.

Built about two years ago.

PENZANCE TOWN GAOL.

Two close rooms: no court-yard: no water.

PRISON of PENWITH at PENZANCE.

'The door had not been opened for four weeks when I went in; and then the Keeper began shoveling away the dirt.'

LOSTWITHIEL GAOL for debtors.

It was lately repaired and whitewashed.

PENRYN GAOL for debtors.

One room.

BODMIN. Two Institutions:

Launceston Castle

Gaols in Bodmin

COUNTY BRIDEWELL for Minor Offenders.

Also known as the 'House of Correction' at Church Stile. After 1779, it became 'Bodmin Brewery'. Demolished 1898.

SHERIFF'S WARD at Bodmin.

Also known as 'The County Prison for Debtors' in Prison Lane. Now the *'Hole in the Wall'*, Public House, Crockwell Street.

1778 Act of Parliament

After the reports on the state of the local prisons, the Justices decided that Cornwall should have a new County Gaol. This was made possible by a private Act of Parliament which was passed in 1778.

ANNO REGNI

GEORGII III.

R E G I S

Magnæ Britanniæ, Franciæ, & Hiberniæ,

DECIMO OCTAVO.

At the Parliament begun and holden at *Westminster*, the Twenty-ninth Day of *November, Anno Domini* 1774, in the Fifteenth Year of the Reign of our Sovereign Lord GEORGE the Third, by the Grace of God, of *Great Britain, France,* and *Ireland*, King, Defender of the Faith, *etc.*

And from thence continued, by several Prorogations, to the Twentieth Day of *November*, 1777; being the Fourth Session of the Fourteenth Parliament of *Great Britain*.

L O N D O N:
Printed by CHARLES EYRE and WILLIAM STRAHAN, Printers to the King's most Excellent Majesty. 1778.

C A P. XVII.

An Act for building an additional Jail, and also a Prison and House of Correction, within the County of *Cornwall*; and for other Purposes therein mentioned.

The Act was granted to the local Justices, for the construction of three new institutions on a new site at Bodmin.

1. **An additional Jail** *(for Felons i.e. a County Gaol for serious offenders)* similar to Launceston.

2. **A Prison** *(At this time, Prison was the institution for Debtors).*

3. **A House of Correction** *(for minor offenders. Later known as a Bridewell).* All within the County of Cornwall;

4. and for other Purposes therein mentioned. (This included the Rights to purchase the land and to build a leat (water course) to bring water from Fairwash to the new buildings).

The Design and Building of the Gaol

Sir John Call, Bart., J.P., M.P., a retired military engineer, designed the new gaol based on *'A Plan for a County Gaol'* published by John Howard, the great prison reformer. An etching was sent to John Howard showing Call's interpretation of the Howard plans.

Sir John Call
(1732-1801)

A PLAN for a COUNTY GAOL.

Front of Gaoler's House & Debtors Ward.

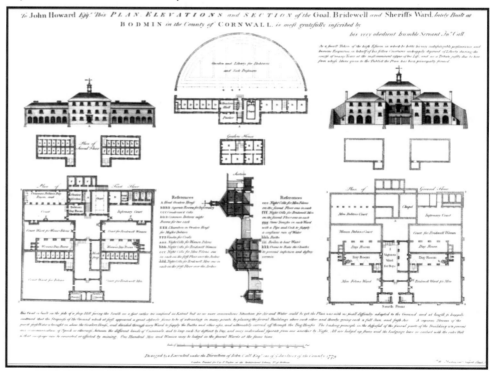

Bodmin Gaol – a Milestone in Prison Design

The design included many new ideas for the humane treatment of prisoners:-

1. Light and airy, and therefore healthy. Individual sleeping cells for prisoners.
2. Different isolated areas for felons, misdemeanants and debtors. Total segregation of males and females
3. Running water in courtyards, boilers for hot water. Ovens to bake clothes (to kill vermin).
4. Useful work for prisoners. Paid for their labour from profits
5. Chapel and Infirmary for sick prisoners

Howard's response to the gaol after his visit to Bodmin in 1782:
"By a spirited exertion, the gentlemen of this county have erected a monument of their humanity, and attention to health and morals of prisoners."

Expansion of Bodmin Gaol

Soon after the gaol opened, the Governor applied to the Justices for changes to be made to individual buildings and their function. This rebuilding/expansion programme continued for many years. The reasons for these changes included:

1. Committals to the gaol increased markedly after the end of the Napoleonic Wars in 1815.

2. The closure of the Old County Gaol at Launceston in 1829.

3. The Gaol Act 1823. This emphasized separate confinement and a five-fold classification of prisoners. **For the Gaol:** *Charged with Felony, Charged with Misdemeanour, Convicted of Felony, Convicted of Misdemeanours, and Debtors.* **In the House of Correction**: Same as the Gaol but Vagrants in place of Debtors. The sexes were to be separated at all times, this meant the gaol required separate accommodation and work facilities for up to twenty different classes of prisoners.

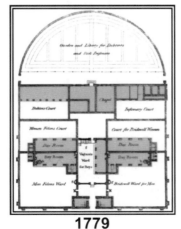

1779

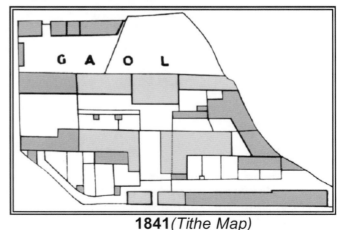

1841(Tithe Map)

Watercolour of the Gaol 1841

This painting is in good agreement with the ground plan (Tithe Map 1841). Two of the original buildings, the Governor's House (*darker colour*) and the adjacent building (*right*) have not changed from the 1779 plan. The area of the gaol has been increased, there are new buildings and the other original buildings have been extended.
By 1850, the Prison Inspectors declared the buildings *'Unfit for Purpose'*. This resulted in a new gaol being built (1856-1861).

Plan of the New Gaol

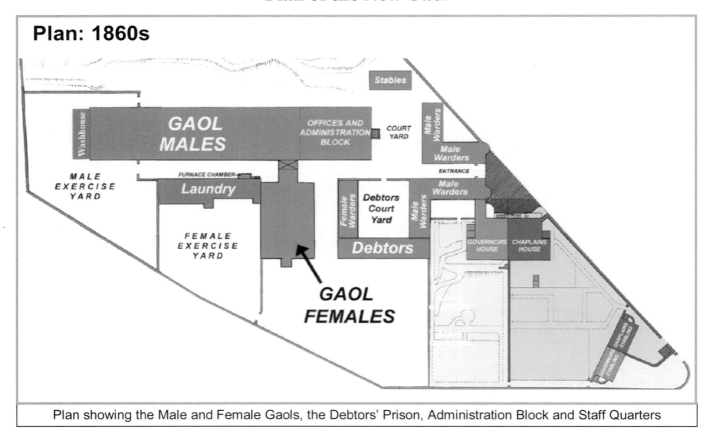

Plan: 1860s

- Stables
- Washhouse
- **GAOL MALES**
- OFFICES AND ADMINISTRATION BLOCK
- COURT YARD
- Male Warders
- *Male Warders*
- MALE EXERCISE YARD
- FURNACE CHAMBER
- Laundry
- ENTRANCE
- Female Warders
- Debtors Court Yard
- *Male Warders*
- *Male Warders*
- FEMALE EXERCISE YARD
- **Debtors**
- GOVERNORS HOUSE
- CHAPLAINS HOUSE
- *GAOL FEMALES*
- CHAPLAINS STERLING
- GOVERNORS STERLING

Plan showing the Male and Female Gaols, the Debtors' Prison, Administration Block and Staff Quarters

Plan of HM Prison, Bodmin & HM Naval Prison

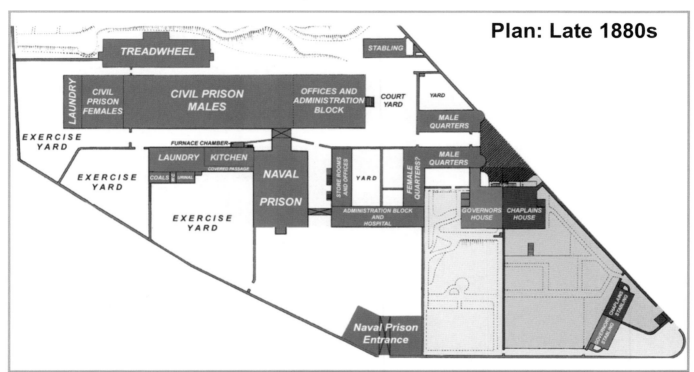

Plan: Late 1880s

TREADWHEEL

STABLING

LAUNDRY

CIVIL PRISON FEMALES

CIVIL PRISON MALES

OFFICES AND ADMINISTRATION BLOCK

COURT YARD

YARD

MALE QUARTERS

EXERCISE YARD

FURNACE CHAMBER

LAUNDRY

KITCHEN

COVERED PASSAGE

COALS

W.C.

URINAL

MALE QUARTERS

EXERCISE YARD

NAVAL PRISON

STORE ROOMS AND OFFICES

YARD

FEMALE QUARTERS?

EXERCISE YARD

ADMINISTRATION BLOCK AND HOSPITAL

GOVERNORS HOUSE

CHAPLAINS HOUSE

GOVERNORS STABLING

CHAPLAINS STABLING

Naval Prison Entrance

All local (County) Gaols were Nationalised in 1877, Cornwall County Gaol became HM Prison, Bodmin. In 1887, the Female block and most of the Debtors' Prison were transferred to the Admiralty for the new Naval Prison. A Naval Prison entrance was built and the Female prisoners were moved to the end of the main Male Civil block.

Position of the Howard Prison

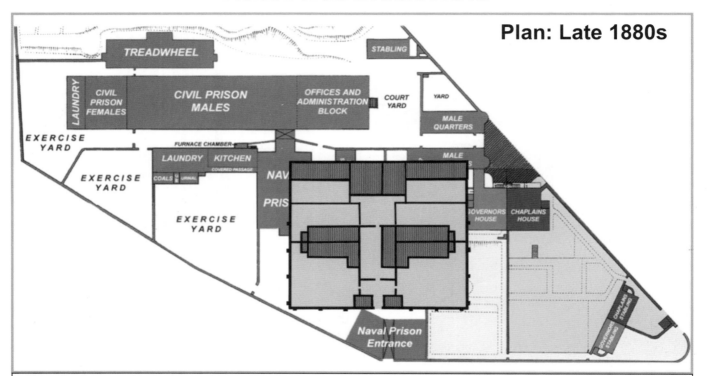

Plan: Late 1880s

TREADWHEEL

LAUNDRY

CIVIL PRISON FEMALES

CIVIL PRISON MALES

OFFICES AND ADMINISTRATION BLOCK

COURT YARD

STABLING

YARD

MALE QUARTERS

EXERCISE YARD

EXERCISE YARD

FURNACE CHAMBER

LAUNDRY KITCHEN

COALS URINAL

COVERED PASSAGE

NAV

PRIS

MALE

EXERCISE YARD

GOVERNORS HOUSE

CHAPLAINS HOUSE

CHAPLAINS STABLING

GOVERNORS STABLING

Naval Prison Entrance

This plan is to scale. It shows the position and size of the 1779 Howard Prison. This position is consistent with reports that the Male block was built while the 'Old Gaol' was still standing. Both male & female prisoners were moved into the male block, the old buildings were then demolished and the female gaol was built.

Bodmin Gaol, about 1900.

Staff Numbers

Originally the gaol was run by a Gaoler with two turnkeys and their families. The Surgeon and Chaplain both lived in the town.

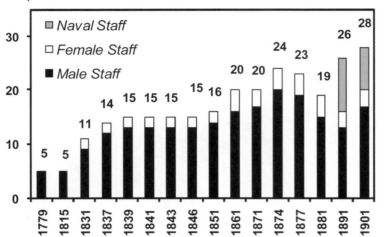

Between 1815 and 1839 the number of staff gradually increased to about 15. The job titles included: Keeper, Chaplain, Surgeon, Matron (responsible for female prisoners), three male and one female Turnkeys, Taskmaster/Shoemaker, Miller, Porter, Watchman, Superintendant of Treadwheel & Schoolmaster (later replaced by Clerk).

When the new gaol was completed the staff numbers increased to about 20. Job titles were changed to: Governor, Chaplain, Surgeon, Clerk, Matron, 6 Male Warders, 2 Assistant Warders, 3 Female Assistant Matrons, 2 Watchmen, Baker and an Engineer. One of the watchmen was later replaced by a Schoolmaster.

The number of staff gradually increased to 24 by 1874. When all local gaols were nationalised in 1877, the staff numbers started to decrease. In 1887, when the Naval Prison was established a new group of staff were employed. The only members of staff shared between the two separate prisons were the Surgeon (Medical Officer) and the Chaplain. The Civil Prison staff increased to 20 by 1901, even though there were very few serious offenders in the prison.

In the early 1900s there were more female staff members than female prisoners.

Governors of the Civil Prison

Governor	From	To	Governor	From	To	Governor	From	To
Edmund Leach	1779?	1780	Hugh G. Colville	1860	1879	Wm. R. Shenton	1896	post1901
James Chapple	1780	1827	Maj. E W Lane	1879	1883	Jas. H.Duncan.	1903	?
Fred. Chapple	1827		Mr Parr	1883		Henry L. Browett	pre1906	1916
John B Everest	1828	1860	William Stevens	1883	1896			

Edmund Leach. In January 1780, he complained that Thomas Jones, the contractor, had not completed the buildings in a proper, workmanlike way. The justices dismissed his complaint as groundless and discharged him from office.

James Chapple, foreman of the builders of the gaol, was appointed temporary gaoler. A post he held for 48 years until his death in 1827. The Justices thought that he was a rogue. He was criticized for not producing accounts and the dubious employment of prisoners.

Frederick Chapple, son of James, was appointed *'Keeper of the Common Gaol'* in October 1827 but at the next Quarter Sessions,

John Bentham Everest, a professional gaoler from Chatham, was appointed Governor. A post he held until his retirement in 1860. Effectively there were only two governors of the gaol between 1780 and 1860. The Inspectors described Everest as *"one of the best of prison governors"* and that *"the County Prison at Bodmin one of the best conducted in England".* Everest was followed by

Governor Colville, who was later promoted to Governor of Wandsworth. Under the new prison system, governors were transferred regularly.

H.L. Browett, The last Governor, retired when the prison closed in 1916.

Bodmin Town Museum

Henry Leonard Browett

Prisoners – Numbers in Civil Prison

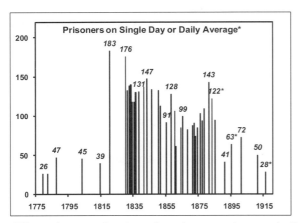

Prisoners on Single Day or Daily Average*

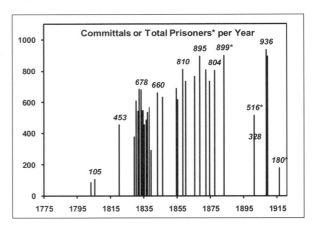

Committals or Total Prisoners* per Year

The above charts, showing gaol population on single days and the total committals or total prisoners per year, contain data for Civil, Army & Navy prisoners and Debtors in the Civil prison.

The increase in the gaol population, between 1815 and 1820, was caused by an increase in the County population and the large number of servicemen, returning from the Napoleonic Wars, seeking work. This crime wave was national. From this peak, the number of prisoners on day counts gradually decreased. The first Army and Navy prisoners arrived in 1874 and continued until the gaol closure.

The number of committals per year, which started to increase around 1820, continued to rise up to 1885 and then started to decline. The peak around 1908 was caused by a crackdown on vagrants.

The decrease in prisoner numbers, which started before 1850, was not due to less crime but to a significant reduction in the number of debtors, more 'Fines' and a significant reduction in the length of sentences handed down by the judges and magistrates.

The Cells

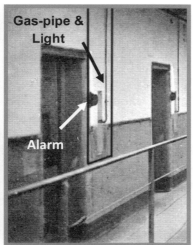

Gas-pipe & Light

Alarm

To be certified, a cell had to be a certain size (13ft. long x 7ft. wide). All the doors were 6ft 3in x 2ft 3in x 2½in thick and lined internally with iron sheets. The sleeping rooms in the Debtors' prison were not certified as cells because of size. They could not be used even when they were transferred to the Navy.

Each cell contained two small corner shelves on the outside wall. There was a list of the allowed contents in a cell. In 1901, it contained the following items: *Bed with wooden slats and mattress. Pillow with slip, sheets, blankets and coverlet rolled-up. Books, including Bible, Prayer book, Hymn book and other allowed books, for example, 'Pilgrim's Progress' by Bunyan.* *Wooden stool. Mirror. 1 gallon can of water. Washing bowl. Slop pot. A salt cellar. Wooden spoon. Cleaning rags for shining-up the metal vessels. Very small hand brush for sweeping. Copy of gaol regulations.*

In the male prison, all cells were lit by a gas light placed outside each cell. A thick piece of glass prevented the prisoner from interfering with the light. The shape of the '*light window*' was tall and narrow. Punishment cells had no lighting, except for the window. A different system was used in the original women's prison, either they were allowed candles or the gas lights were inside the cells.

Outside each cell was a device, which could be activated by a prisoner requiring assistance. By pulling a lever, a bell would ring near the warder's room and an indicator would be raised outside the cell.

The Heating & Ventilation System

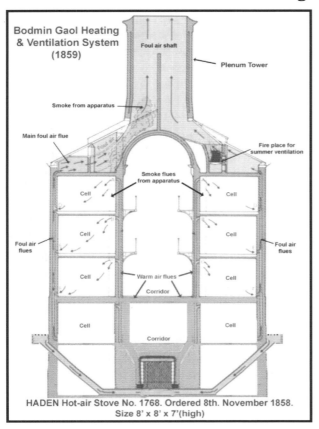

Bodmin Gaol Heating & Ventilation System (1859)

Foul air shaft

Plenum Tower

Smoke from apparatus

Main foul air flue

Fire place for summer ventilation

Smoke flues from apparatus

Cell — Cell

Foul air flues

Cell — Cell

Foul air flues

Cell — Cell

Warm air flues

Corridor

Cell — Cell

Corridor

HADEN Hot-air Stove No. 1768. Ordered 8th. November 1858. Size 8' x 8' x 7'(high)

It is a little surprising to find that prisons from the early 1840s were built with heating and ventilation systems which kept the temperature in every cell between 12° and 15° C both in the Winter and Summer.

The heating was provided by cold air travelling between the inner and outer cases of a hot-air stove, which was placed in the basement of the building. The warmed air was then distributed to every cell by ducts inside the cell walls. Stale air was removed by ducts in the outside walls of the cells into the plenum tower. Each cell also contained a fresh air inlet. In Summer the stove would not be used but a fire would be made in a fire-room in the roof of the building which would draw outside air though each cell and out via the tower.

The diagram, dated 8th November, 1858, copied from the Order Book of Haden's of Trowbridge, shows the details of the main male-block heating stove.

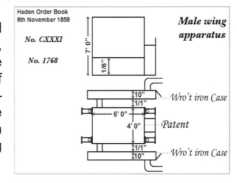

Haden Order Book 8th November 1858

No. CXXXI

No. 1768

Male wing apparatus

7' 0"

1/6"

10"

1/1"

Wro't iron Case

6' 0"

Patent

4' 0"

1/1"

10"

Wro't iron Case

Employment of Prisoners

At the end of the eighteenth century, prison was solely for the detention of offenders and not a place of punishment. This meant that the gaol could be used as a commercial, profit making concern. All prisoners could do useful work, which earned money for the county, the gaoler and the prisoner. The work for men consisted of cutting and polishing stone and slate, cutting wood, shoemaking and working in the garden. The women were employed in spinning, weaving and knitting. The gaoler would supply the raw materials and sell the finished objects.

In the early nineteenth century the prison system came under criticism, it was thought that it did not deter criminals from re-offending. Useless labour was considered a great deterrent because the prisoner hated it for its uselessness; indeed, it was even argued that the knowledge that his work accomplished nothing had a reformative effect. These new ideas were accepted by the governor and led to the introduction of the two treadwheels and other hard labour machines in 1824.

www.learnhistory.org.uk

In the mid 1850s, prisoners at Bodmin worked on the building of the new gaol. By 1865, the main hard-labour task was Oakum Picking: unravelling pieces of old rope into individual filaments. This was sold to ship-yards where it was mixed with tar and used for caulking wooden ships.

After the Prison Act of 1865, a new Treadwheel was built. Prisoners worked four hours and rested four hours by alternate periods of 15 minutes, ascending 7,800-12,000 feet per day. During rest prisoners were employed picking oakum. This regime continued until the Prison Act of 1898 abolished the Treadwheel and ruled that all work should be productive. Back to the Beginning!

Prison Diets

1782: 1lb. 3oz. of *'good wholesome bread'* per day and 1lb. for women. All prisoners who attended divine service on Saturday were allowed ½lb. of meat made into broth for dinner on Sunday.

1823: The Gaol Act of ordered the following diet: *All prisoners shall be provided with the following diet:- Two lbs. bread, 2 oz. cheese and one onion for four days in the week, and 2 lbs. of bread, ¾ lb. suet puddings, three days in the week. For those prisoners who shall be for twelve months and upwards: as above, and after the twelve months an additional pint of beer per week.* This dietary was ignored by local authorities and even ten years later, different gaols still had different diets. The diet at the County Gaol at Bodmin was cited for having one of the worst diets in the country. *"... at the Cornwall County Gaol, at Bodmin, the daily ration was, for the first month, only a pound-and-a-half of bread, with the addition, after that period, of a portion of gruel."* The diet at Bodmin was improved after this criticism by the addition of potatoes and soup.

1874: The diet for prisoners was dependent on the length of Sentence and was increased for Hard Labour. *Part of the 1874 Diet is reproduced below:*

CLASS 1			CLASS 3			CLASS 5		
Prisoners confined for any Term not exceeding 14 Days.			Prisoners for Terms between 1 Month and 2 Months.			Prisoners at Hard Labour above Six Months.		
	Males over 16	Males <16 & Women		Males over 16	Males <16 & Women		Males over 16	Males <16 & Women
Breakfast and Supper	1 pint gruel	1 pint gruel	Breakfast and Supper	1 pint gruel, 6 oz. bread	1 pint gruel, 6 oz. bread	Breakfast and Supper	1 pint gruel, 8 oz. bread	1 pint gruel, 6 oz. bread
Dinner	1 lb. bread	1 lb. bread	Dinner 4 days	2 oz. Meat 1 lb. potatoes	2 oz. Meat 12 oz. potatoes	Dinner 4 days	4 oz. Meat 1 lb. potatoes 6 oz. bread	3 oz. Meat 1 lb. potatoes 4 oz. bread
			Dinner 3 days	⅔ pint soup 1 lb. potatoes	⅔ pint soup 12 oz. potatoes	Dinner 3 days	1 pint soup 1 lb. potatoes 6 oz. bread	1 pint soup 1lb. potatoes 4 oz. bread

1911: Diet more varied than earlier but the quantity of food provided still depended on the length of the prisoner's sentence. Less meat but suet pudding, fat bacon, beans and tea were added.

Other Sentences of the Courts

In addition to sending convicted prisoners to gaol or giving a Fine, the Judges and Magistrates could add additional punishments and even more serious sentences.

Solitary Confinement: This sentence was rare. The punishment was limited to two weeks, for example, for a 1 month sentence in gaol, only the first and last week would be in solitary.

Hard Labour: The percentage of prisoners at Hard Labour increased from 42% in 1816 to 91% in the 1830s. It was in the range 42-57% in the 1840s and later in the century, under the Four Stage System, all fit prisoners did the equivalent of Hard Labour at the start of their sentence.

Whipping: Very common sentence before 1850. After 1830 usually carried out in private.

1812 Quarter Sessions:
John Chapman, who stole one gallon of wheat, was sentenced to two years hard labour, during which time on two market days, public whipping in streets of Bodmin *'from Butter Market 100 yards up the street unless he shall in the meantime voluntarily enter into his Majesty's army.'*

Transportation: Sending convicts to the colonies was an alternative punishment to hanging for felons. The American War (1778-83) prevented the government from sending convicts to America and the government had to accommodate about 1000 extra convicts per year. The simple solution was to house the convicts in the ships previously used as transports. Planned as a temporary measure, the use of prison hulks lasted until 1858, even though Australia was conveniently discovered in 1770 and the penal colony of Botany Bay was established in 1788. After 1857 transportation was replaced by

Penal Servitude: Total isolation, restricted diet, plank bed & *'deprivation of all humanising privileges'.*

Death: Execution by hanging.

Executions in Cornwall (1735-1909)

The Route to the Scaffold

(1)

(2)

(3)

From the original condemned cell on the lower ground floor (1), the prisoner was taken into the corridor (2) via the 'secret door', usual covered by a wardrobe. He would cross the floor into corridor (3). It is not known if there were additional walls between (2) and (3).
He would be taken through the door (4) past the female prison to the 'drop' on the south wall.

(4)

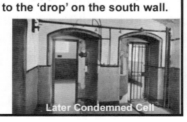
Later Condemned Cell

THE CRIMES		
Murder	33	(1735-1909)
Infanticide	7	(1742-1878)
Burglary	13	(1735-1828)
Highway Robbery	7	(1741-1795)
Stealing:		
Horse	3	(1741-1791)
Sheep	5	(1742-1818)
Wreck	1	(1767)
Ox	1	(1791)
Wheat	1	(1796)
Money	1	(1798)
Ram	1	(1820)
Killing mare	1	(1791)
Forgery	2	(1801 & 1812)
Arson (Corn stack)	2	(1813 & 1825)
Robbery violence	1	(1827)
Bestiality	1	(1834)
TOTAL	**80**	

EXECUTIONS		
Launceston	8	(1735-1821)
St Stephens	2	(1767 & 1793)
BODMIN	60	(1755-1909)
Date/Place?	8B + 1L + 1?	(1735-1748)

Places of Execution in Bodmin

1735 – 1802:	By gibbet on Bodmin Common (St. Lawrence Site).
1802 – 1828:	By drop gallows, outside wall of old gaol.
1834 – 1909:	On the gaol site. Three different places.

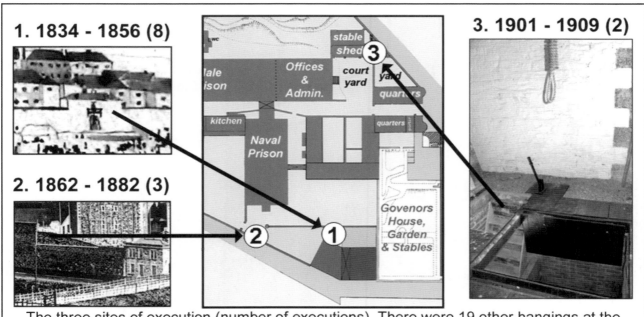

The three sites of execution (number of executions). There were 19 other hangings at the gaol but outside the walls (1802-1828).

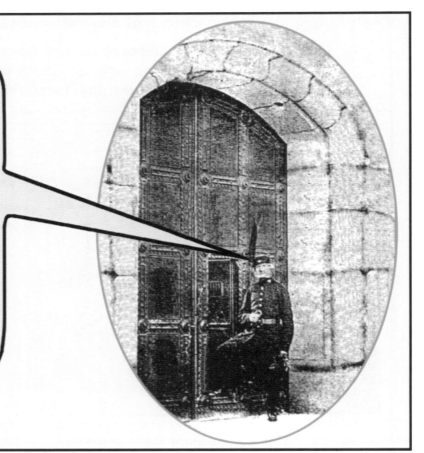

In 1887 parts of the Civil Prison were transferred to the Admiralty for use as H.M. Naval Prison.

Naval Prisoners in Bodmin Prison

The Royal Navy sent naval prisoners to Devonport Borough Prison to serve their sentences. In 1873, The local Admiral of the Fleet, Sir Henry Keppel wrote to the Admiralty: *I have the honour to request that you will be pleased to direct their Lordships' attention to the accompanying unsatisfactory report on the Devonport Borough Prison, showing that our men return to duty physically deteriorated, from insufficient dietary, and morally, by faulty discipline in points of cleanliness and occupation, and by association with the rogues and vagrants of a large district.*

The Admiralty agreed and decided to send prisoners to Bodmin Prison, which at that time was run by Governor Colville, 'a military officer of over 20 years service'. From Autumn 1874, all naval prisoners from Courts Martial on the flagship *'Royal Adelaide'* at Devonport, served their sentences at Bodmin.

HMS Royal Adelaide

Admiral of the Fleet The Hon. Sir HENRY KEPPEL, C.G.B.

Establishment of HM Naval Prison, Bodmin

In the 1880s Bodmin Prison, was too large for the number of prisoners being sentenced. The Prison Commissioners offered parts of the Prison to the Admiralty. Two buildings, the Debtors' Prison, not used after 1869, and the Women's Prison, which had few prisoners, were transferred to the Navy. The new Naval Prison opened in 1877/8.

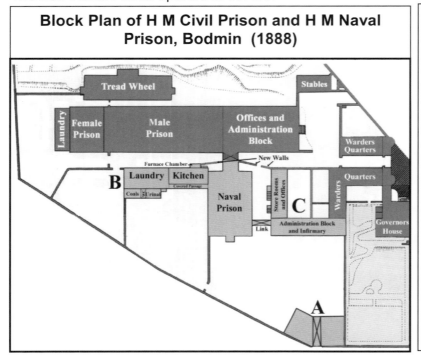

Block Plan of H M Civil Prison and H M Naval Prison, Bodmin (1888)

Labels within plan: Tread Wheel; Stables; Laundry; Female Prison; Male Prison; Offices and Administration Block; Warders Quarters; Furnace Chamber; New Walls; Quarters; Warders; **B**; Laundry; Kitchen; Covered Passage; Coals; Urinal; Store Rooms and Offices; **C**; Naval Prison; Administration Block and Infirmary; Link; Governors House; **A**

CHANGES TO CIVIL PRISON:

Loss of the Debtors' Prison.

New Laundry converted from old washhouse.

New Female prison at the end of the main block.

NEW NAVAL PRISON:

Main Building: Naval Block previously the Female Prison.

Building **'A'**: Gatekeepers Lodge, reception, entrance with inner & outer gates and Warders Quarters.

Building **'B'**: New Kitchen & Laundry converted from female laundry.

Building **'C'**: Offices for Governor, Clerk, Chaplain, Surgeon, Chief Warder, etc.

Governor's Residence was never built. All the Governors lived in the town.

Services: WC's, latrines, coal stores etc., were built onto building **'B'**.

Life in the Naval Prison

Under the 'Naval Discipline Act' only prisoners who were to remain in the service, were imprisoned in the naval prison. Those prisoners, whose sentence included dismissal from the navy, had to be held in a civil prison.

The philosophy of the naval prison system was that every prisoner should be made to feel that his state and condition in prison was worse than when he was on active service. They worked very hard, received basic food, were frequently reminded of their sins by the Chaplain, discipline was severe and their daily life was ruled by the *'silent system'*. The main objective of this regime was to prevent re-offending.

In general, the working week and time-tables were similar to those in the Civil Prison. The diet for navy prisoners contained extra meat as it had been shown that the standard prison diet resulted in navy men losing weight and being unfit for work when they returned to the fleet. Work consisted of Oakum picking, Treadwheel and the Navy exercise called 'Shot Drill'.

Shot Drill

Shot exercise performed with a 24lb shot. The shot was placed in two lines, or in the form of a rectangle, from six to eight paces apart. The men fell in, each with a shot in front of him. On a given word, the men stoop and lift the shot, so that the elbows and shot should be level with the hips, and move briskly to the next position. On a signal, the shot is placed on the floor, the man comes to attention, and, on command, marches back to his original position. This procedure is repeated for a period of 1.5hrs. The maximum for shot exercise is 3 hours per day.

The whole of this exercise was timed. For example, if the shot was placed six paces apart, the shot was moved at a rate of 5 per minute. This meant that 1,800 paces were marched with shot and 1,800 paces without shot in one hour.

This exercise was changed to a punishment by increasing the shot weight to 32lbs. and changing the routine so that the prisoner did not march back to his original position but always continued to the next position. In the above example, this meant that the prisoner carried the shot for 3,600 paces in one hour.

Prisoners were permitted in warm weather to remove their jackets. If a prisoner stopped during the exercise, he was to continue for 10 minutes, for each stop, after the class was dismissed, unless the Medical Officer certified that it was unavoidable.

The Civil Prison was not used after 1916 and the Naval Prison closed in 1922. All buildings sold in 1929.

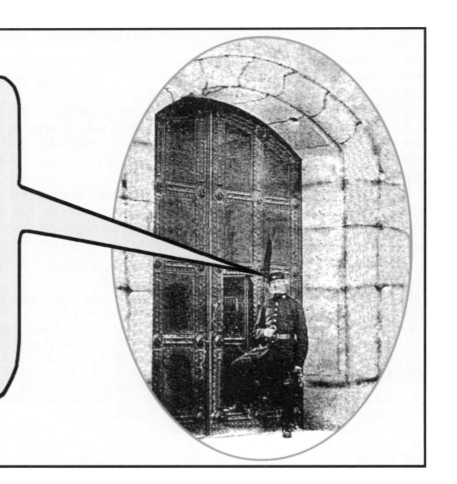

Closure of the Prisons

1911: The female part of the gaol was closed.

1915: *'Owing to the low number of persons now being committed to prison they have made arrangements to temporarily close the establishment at Bodmin on the 1st June next.'*

5th Feb 1918 – 25th February 1919: Storage of both State Papers and Records. *'The heating was off but it is considered that while traces of mildew are in evidence, the books and rolls have suffered no permanent damage'.*

1922: The Naval Prison ceased to be used.

1927: Gaol was formally closed.

1929: The buildings were sold as Lots. For example, the Governor's House, Chaplaincy, Naval quarters and Warders' quarters were sold to individuals. The gaol and the remainder of the land were sold to Mr A. S. Lee of Ipswich for £1,050. The Total for all the lots was £4,340.

Sale Plan (1929)

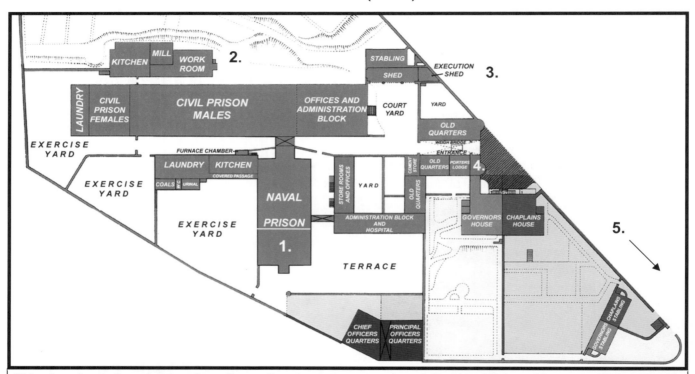

This plan shows five changes from the earlier plans: the extension of the Naval Prison (1); a new kitchen, hand-mill room & work room in the old Treadwheel building (2); the building of an execution shed (3); Porter's Lodge with weighbridge in part of the old quarters (4) and off-site Warders' Quarters (5).

Gaol Image 1930

Shortly after the sale of the gaol, the Vandals moved in. This image shows some of the buildings being demolished. 1. The hole in the main wall; 2. The roof of the naval infirmary and stores (old Debtors' Prison) has been removed; 3. Part of the old quarters is being demolished.

Gaol Image 2006

Civil Prison Block

Naval Prison Block

Entertainment at Bodmin Jail

THE "99" CLUB

THE OLD PRISON
- BODMIN -

'THE CLINK WITH A DRINK'

Have You a convict's number ? ? ?
If not, You are cordially invited to apply for same at the above !!!!

Open Mornings 11.30 a.m. — 2 p.m.
Evenings 7.0 p.m. — 11.30 p.m.

FULLY LICENSED BARS

Eastern Cocktail Lounge   Running Buffet

We offer you Nightly Dancing in the famous Old Chapel
Ballroom with its Super Deal Floor

SPACIOUS DINING ROOM

Book your tables for Lunch and Dinner (available April 1st. 1947)
PARTIES CATERED FOR

★ You'll never want ' BAIL ' when you come to our ' JAIL ' !! ★

BODMIN JAIL

MEMBERSHIP CARD

NAME

Expires 31st May 1972

N.º 574

BODMIN JAIL NIGHT CLUB & CASINO

OLD BODMIN PRISON. Bodmin 2999

Come to Cornwall's gayest Night Spot—the only place in Cornwall where you can see two different first-class Cabaret acts twice nightly, seven nights a week, and DANCING!

TONIGHT, FRIDAY AND SATURDAY :
PAUL DANIELS
Must be one of the best comedians and magicians in the business.

Also STRIPTEASE by
FARINA

☆ DANCING every night to **Bob Cooks Trio**

Admission :
Tonight and Friday —
4/- members, 6/- guests
Sat., Sun. and Mon.—
6/- members, 8/6 guests
Tue. to Fri. inclusive—
4/- members, 6/- guests

RESTAURANT
open every night

SUNDAY NIGHT AND ALL NEXT WEEK :

Another big attraction to the club — Radio and TV Star (who you all must know) :
VINCE EAGER

Also STRIPTEASE by that well-known
MAI LOO

Special attraction on Monday next :
ROD MASON and The Tamar Valley Jazz Band

Since WWII, the Administration Block, which includes the Chapel, has been used as a Night-Club, Casino, bars and restaurants. The ephemera shown above, date from 1946 to 1972.

Top: Repairs to the Chapel roof and new ceiling and windows. *Bottom Centre:* Image shows the extensive damage at the top of the tower. *Bottom Left:* Getting to the top & *Bottom right:* After the repairs.

Repairs & Renovations (2)

Major Changes to Restaurants and Bars: *Top left:* Refurbishment of the main bar. *Top Right:* New lounge and Cocktail Bar. *Other Images:* The logo and views of the new *'La Scala'* restaurant created in the old prison chapel. The balconies above the curved entrance are the original seating areas for the Governor and his Staff.

Other Bodmin Attractions

CORNWALL'S REGIMENTAL MUSEUM

BODMIN & WENFORD RAILWAY

BEACON NAT. RES.

LANHYDROCK HOUSE

SHIRE HALL (OLD ASSIZES COURT)

PENCARROW HOUSE

ST. PETROC'S CH.

BODMIN TOWN MUSEUM

The
ripple of dementia

WWW.APPLEBYBOOKS.CO.UK

Joanne Appleby

First Published 2020

Text ©2020 Joanne Appleby

The right of Joanne Appleby to be identified
as author of this work has been asserted by her in accordance with the Copyright,
Designs and Patents Act 1988.

www.applebybooks.co.uk

Reprographics and Printing by:
Beamreach Printing (www.beamreachuk.co.uk)

ISBN 978-1-5272-7359-7

Contents

Dedication

Dedicated to my Mam and Dad, who passed away within 16 days of each other in January and February 2019, having both suffered neurological diseases of Vascular Dementia and Parkinson's disease.

60 years of marriage and best friends,

Thank you for everything,

Joanne xx

Introduction

Everyone has different coping strategies when dealing with bereavement and loss.

My poems and words are written from the heart and are an attempt to show with honesty and reality, my thoughts about bereavement and loss.

At times, my words are raw in their immediacy, hopefully the reader will be able to relate to my words and ultimately this may be helpful.

We all suffer loss at some point in our lives, how we deal with it is key to how we cope.

For me, personally, I do not think you ever really move on, you just learn to live your daily life whatever form that may take. Emotions are highly complex.

I hope you find your way.

You never really think that your parents will die. As a child you think they will live forever.

When the roles are reversed and you start to look after them, a change occurs that in turn changes who you are and what your life will be without them.

For some, looking after loved ones can be very challenging coping with the daily demands that serious illness brings.

For me, being in touch with reality helped, I knew what was coming and I knew what to expect.

Seeing my Mother and Father deteriorate at the same time was cruel not only for them but for the family too.

My Dad who suffered from Parkinson's Disease for over 25 years was very much aware of what was happening until the last couple of months, however, at times his body shook uncontrollably and he was trapped in the "life in prison" sentence that the disease gave him.

For my mother, it was different, as Vascular Dementia had taken its toll over the years and therefore, she was not aware of what was going on for the last year or two. Her routine was simple, at times, childlike.

Dementia sufferers say some weird and at times some wonderful things, which make you smile or make you sad. My Mam was particularly funny when she started to swear! It was so strange to hear her say "bloody" as all through my years with her, she had never used any bad language of any kind and was a very mild mannered woman.

One of the saddest things I ever heard my Mam say whilst trying to get her to eat her lunch, was the sentence " It's too dangerous to eat". From that moment, I knew it was the beginning of the end. Dementia had cast its final blow and planted the seed. Mam always loved her food and was a good eater! Those are not words she would have spoken. From that day on, many attempts at trying to coax her to eat failed, not even her favourite Battenberg finger cakes would tempt her. At times she would ask for a cup of tea or water, however, after only a couple of sips, she claimed she was full.

The end was approaching as dementia changed gear.

The Ripple of Dementia

As I look into the water, I see no reflection, for I have disappeared forever into the depths of the unknown.

A reflection does not always tell the truth, but ripples and skirts around the edges, perhaps distorting reality.

Do not chase the ripple, it no longer exists, and dilutes itself further and further in a quest never to be discovered.

The deep waters of Dementia know no bounds, they will flow free as you remain stagnant. Until the drought begins.

Are You ?

Are you looking after me now that I don't know who I am?

Tell me, what do you see when you look at me, do you still see your Mam?

My thoughts may be broken and taken from me, my eyes may stare at you, so tell me what do you see?

Take comfort in the fact that I am still your Mother, I carried you, gave birth to you and loved you from the start.

The ravages of disease may have robbed me of my thoughts, but my heart is full of love, that I give to you with ease.

Do not be sad and weep, for I have left you with lots of memories, you will think of as I sleep.

Still my Dad

As I looked at you Dad, I could hardly recognise you. Your body stiffened and shaken, your control slowly taken, leaving you entombed.

For you to know what was happening made me sick to the stomach.

How a good man could be punished so harshly was beyond me.

Still, when I looked at you, the good man was still there, at times I got a glimpse and I knew you were there.

You had a lifetime together with Mam and four children too.

Your values and decency over the years always shone through.

As I write these words for all to see, you will always be my Dad, and I thank you for the life we had.

Wait for me Dad

Saturday afternoon and it was time to leave, I whispered into your ear "wait for me Dad".

I was heading home, some two hundred miles away but I would return on the Monday.

Monday came and I headed back to you, the phone call came and it was imminent, my thoughts were with you.

I arrived two hours later, and you had waited for me.

As I held your hand, and played your favourite music, you gave your last gasp content in the knowledge that I was there.

I whispered into your ear for the very last time, I made promises to you that will last my lifetime.

I told you not to worry about me and I thanked you for the memories that you had given to me, and for the fact that you had indeed waited for me.

I Never Told You Mam

I never told you Mam that Dad had passed away. I never told you that your soulmate had lived his final day.

Even though you suffered from Dementia and didn't know who or where you were, I could not take the risk of breaking your heart, now that you and your soulmate were finally apart.

You never called his name again until the night before you passed, somewhere in your heart you knew it would be your last.

Only 16 days apart, and now you were back with your sweetheart.

I am glad I never told you Mam, so glad I never broke your heart.

Now you both lie side by side together Mam, in the village where you were born.

60 years of marriage, friendship, and memories too.

As you both look over the river and fields and watch me visit and go, I will feel you as the gentle breeze blows.

The Seasons of Your Life

I never thought I would lose you twice, the hardest was the first.

The seasons were changing, your Dementia remaining and slowly getting worse.

Your journey was coming to an end with all of us trying to comprehend how and when that would be.

You lived the seasons of your life so well. It was a shame the last one was a living hell.

It was time to lose you "twice". So sad your final season, left you without rhyme or reason, only a vacant stare and a silence that showed you were not there.

As you slipped gently away, I whispered in your ear to say sorry that your final season had ended.

All of the seasons we had together, all of the happy and sad times too will remind me of you.

Our bond will never be broken, not even by your passing. For the love you have given for all of our seasons will be part of my life the whole way through. I will always be your Daughter Mam, for that I thank you.

I am Sorry

I am sorry Mam and Dad, that you had to suffer. It made me so sad to see you both struggle through my teary eyes.

It is hard to understand at times, why good people have to suffer.

My only comfort is that you both loved each other.

Every tear I shed for you both, I do not regret. I take comfort in the fact that I was loved for many years. Nor do I regret the daily thoughts of you both that consume my mind.

The flashbacks are very vivid and let me feel what it is like to love and to have been loved.

Dementia has no friends

Dementia has no friends, but it knows a lot of people. It is keen to know more too.

Dementia does not care what you look like, nor does it care where you live or how old you are.

It will happily be your companion and hang out with you for many years.

It will never leave you, and it will take you along for the ride knowing full well your journey will end with not a thought or a care in sight.

Because you see, you are in fact its victim and not its friend.

What a loser you are

Thank you, Dementia, for making me see how fortunate I was. Of course, I despise you for making my mother suffer, but you are the loser by far.

You played your game and sowed your seeds in your quest for supremacy.

Your only victory is being the master of hollowness.

Oh, what a loser you are.

Just one thing you did not expect, my Mother's heart did not forget. A true Mother from the start, and that, Dementia you can never tear apart.

Oh, what a loser you are.

Dignity

As humans we have very little else apart from our own dignity.

We tend to concentrate on our personal possessions or how much money we may or may not have. We strive to buy things we like and the things that will apparently make us happy. In some cases, we insure them against loss.

One thing we cannot insure in our lives is our dignity. It is truly the last thing that we possess as a person.

Once a person's dignity starts to fade through illness, they are very much reliant upon others to help them maintain whatever they have left.

Dignity is truly precious.

Illness and disease does not respect dignity and will strive to extract every last ounce a person has.

Do not think you have failed when trying to help a loved one maintain their dignity.

The very fact that you have tried is, in itself, an act of delivering dignity to someone less fortunate than yourself. You may not feel or ever see much success, but your act shows you cared enough to try.

About the author

I was born and raised in the small village of Rothbury in Northumberland. My Mother was also born and raised in Rothbury.

My Father was born in the nearby village of Longhorsley.

My parents met at the local dance hall in Rothbury village in 1956 after my Dad's family moved into the village.

They married 3 years later in 1959, both aged 21. From that day on they were never apart and remained very happily married for 60 years.

Although it was a very difficult time losing both parents within 16 days of each other to horrible Neurological diseases, I have many lovely memories of my parents, the main one being that they doted on each other and had a very happy life together.

As a family, we grew up in very different times. A lot of people would dearly love to go back to that way of life I am sure!

I try not to remember them as being ill, but the times when we had great summers and picturesque winters together, all of them different in their own way.

I now reside in the Cheshire area and live a quiet life. I enjoy sports in particular swimming and running through woods in the very early morning!

Being in the moment in the woods and listening to the sounds of the birds, often reminds me of adventures we had as kids in Northumberland.

I still have family members in Rothbury, and I visit my parents resting place in the village on a regular basis.

Although there are many differences in the village now, it still holds that familiarity we all tend to crave and find comfort In.

Thank you for reading my work and I wish you well,

Joanne Appleby

Other books by the author

Joanne Appleby is also the author of ...

I am your daughter Mam

also the children's story book

Bobby the Allotment Robin

All books are available on Amazon and other online sites,
and are also available on the author's website at

www.applebybooks.co.uk

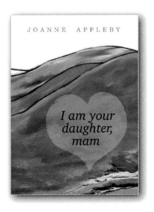